" ' Preserve an agnostic silence about them,' says John Robinson, the Suffragan Bishop of Woolwich, ' since they cannot be painted with the assurance or the detail of the wide canvases beloved of our forefathers.' Followers of Dr. Tillich simply ignore dogmas that do not relate to modern man's ultimate concern. Many cry out ' Demythologise!', others crave to do away with ' the devil ' and his court. In other words, all churches and their thinkers have come to realise that there must be a change, a ' renewal ' if the church is again to have any meaning to modern man.

" It must be emphasised that this ' renewal ' is still as yet an intellectual movement within the churches themselves. To the majority of Christian churchgoers, themselves a minority, religion still implies sacraments and the Bible, believing in the truths of divine revelation, and so on. The miracle-angled belief in the ' divine paradox ' still prevails.

" But the reason for the widespread anguish and despair felt in the most affluent society in history remains the inability to answer the three vital questions of our existence : Where did we come from? What are we doing here? Where are we going?

" Western thought, philosophy, religion and theology all stem from the old Hebrew cosmology as outlined in the Bible. God created it all, and man is the next highest being after Him. With man the centre of such a system, it is basic that Earth is the centre of life in the Universe, and even if these concepts are worded differently today as a consequence of the findings of modern palæontology, Western thought remains steadfastly tied to two basic concepts: human life exists only on this planet; and each individual has only one life to lead, starting at birth and ending at death. After that, there is the eternal, rewarding life of the soul. Perhaps.

" This concept of our place in the Universe is not the result of scientific development of knowledge, through the accumulation of data by observation and measurement: it was derived from what astronomer Fred Hoyle, one of the most brilliant minds of the century, describes as an ' arbitrary starting point '—the so-called divine revelations.

"Says Hoyle in *Frontiers of Astronomy*: 'This procedure is quite characteristic of primitive peoples who, in attempting to explain the local behaviour of the physical world, are obliged in their ignorance of the laws of physics to have recourse to arbitrary starting conditions. These are given credence by postulating the existence of gods—gods of the sea who determine the arbitrary starting conditions that control the motions of the ocean, gods of the mountains, gods of the forest . . . and so forth. . . . There is a strong hint that what modern man is trying to do with the Universe is no better than what primitive man did with problems whose nature we now find simple.' Hoyle was speaking of 'the big bang theory' and others prevailing in modern cosmology. Yet his words could not be more apposite to describe our general attitude towards what we may call spiritual cosmology: we still think in terms of the Hebrew sages of old simply because the 'arbitrary starting conditions' contained in the Bible have been defined as divine revelations or miracles, and are therefore not subject to tests or observation. In other words, there is a gap of three thousand years between our scientific thinking and our religious thinking, centred around the old miracle concept.

"The Temple of Universal Religion is an attempt to close this gap.

"What we have to offer and what we base our actions upon is a working hypothesis in the scientific sense, whose value—as with all scientific theory—depends upon the possibility of disproving it. As T. Gold of Cambridge put it: 'For a theory to be valuable, it must be vulnerable.' The hypothesis is offered as an instrument with which we may attempt to answer those three vital queries of our existence."

And here we must come out from behind the quotation marks, reveal that the writer of this book is in fact the founder and head of the Temple of Universal Religion, discard the editorial plural and adopt the first person, and take responsibility for the hypothesis mentioned above.

What follows is necessarily only a general outline: to expound a detailed and scholarly apologia for the theory

would itself require a whole book. It may therefore be convenient if I state the basic principles of the Temple of Universal Religion, expanding them where it seems necessary with supplementary material.

1. *God is supreme love and supreme wisdom. He expresses Himself through energy that sustains the Universe and is a constantly creative force.*

It is the continual emission of energy from God, which adopts many forms and types, that explains the " continuous origin of matter ". God is neither a fixed point nor a personality, nor (as the Bible would have us believe) does He ever rest. Nothing is at rest. The atom is not at rest: there is always at least one electron moving around a proton at incredible speed in any atom. If God " rested " for a billionth of a second, the entire Universe would disintegrate.

2. *The Universe is expanding, and everything that exists is ruled by the law of evolution.*

The expanding Universe—what Hoyle calls " a decisive reorientation on man's outlook . . . one of the most important scientific revolutions of thought of all time "—is, I think, a sufficiently proven scientific fact to be accepted without qualification. As to how it was created—you can choose the " big bang " theory, the theory of the continuous creation cosmologists, or the most recent hypothesis of Professor William H. McCrea of the University of London's Holloway College, that matter is created in the dense centre of galaxies. The fact is that matter *is* created and science cannot tell how as yet. This is as far as science can go.

Accepting the expanding Universe theory, it can be seen that life on earth follows similar dynamics of expansion which we call evolution. All animal life stems from the original one-cell organism, the amœba, which developed by evolution from the primordial protein cell. Both the super-small and the super-large have one thing in common therefore: dynamic evolution and dynamic expansion. Indeed, Hoyle has spoken of " so far unperceived connections between the physics of the ultra-small and the physics of the ultra-large."

We thus get a picture of a Universe continuously dynamic throughout its vast range.

3. *There are several degrees of condensation of energy. The spiritual world is less condensed than its respective material world. There are an infinite number of worlds and consequently an infinite number of different stages of spiritual and material evolution.*

A basic principle here is that material energy, the one that is known to science, is only a condensation of spiritual energy. The dynamic constitution of material laws, or the laws of nature as they are called, are therefore a consequence of spiritual laws. If one imagines the unbelievable energy that has been found to exist in quasars, for instance, and then reflects that this is but the condensation of the spiritual energy which originated them, one begins to comprehend something of the power of the latter.

The problem is how to explain the condensation of spiritual energy into material energy, how Supreme Love can condense itself down the scale, as it were, until it shows in the ultra-small atoms that form the primordial cell, then to develop again through millions of years of evolution to form *Homo sapiens.* This is a problem our present stage of intelligence is just not sophisticated enough to understand. But science is progressing at a fantastic pace. . . .

4. *Man is a particle of the Supreme Energy, created with undeveloped faculties which are developed through evolution, directed by his free-will.*

The question is often asked, and has been referred to in an earlier chapter, why, if everything is an expression of Supreme Love, there should exist poverty, misery, hunger and evil generally? If there were a God, how could he permit such things? This is not, as might at first appear, another divine paradox. The answer is: man's free-will. Could there be any real love without free-will? Or, in other words, would an *imposed* love in any sense at all be satisfactory? Of course not: the only validity love can have is if it is *felt* and freely

given; without that, by definition it is not love at all! So once we accept that " love makes the world go round ", quite literally, it follows that the dynamic principle must stem from free-will, free initiative. In matter, this free-will is expressed through evolution, intelligent evolution, which shows a purpose in everything. " The Universe begins to look more like a great thought than like a great machine," Sir James Jeans said in *The Mysterious Universe.*

Our galaxy is about 6,000 million years old. Life on Earth as we know it took some 1,000 million years to evolve, man as he is today around 50,000 years. The free-will or evolution accomplishing this adds an extra dimension for man: the soul. My working hypothesis is that the soul is an individual particle of spiritual energy, endowed with intelligence in a completely primitive stage. It was created by God (to use an image that is intelligible) much as, in matter, the primordial cell was created. How, we cannot say: like the scientist who says, " When a neutron changes to a proton by a β-process an electron is disgorged . . . the electron originates ", we just have to say, " it happens, according to an α process " . . . .

The energy with which the " primordial " soul is initially charged might be expressed by the formula $(E=alw)\infty$, where a is the age of the spirit, l is the love it can develop, and w the wisdom it can acquire. In other words, it has a beginning, but there is no end to the possibility of its evolution, which is infinite (or eternal).

This particle, through electro-magnetic energy continuously spurred by the intelligent principle, starts building round it a physical body in accordance with the conditions of the planet where the process takes place. Here it has so far progressed from the primordial cell to the present body of man (an evolution reflected and repeated in the nine months gestation, from cell to complete foetus, in every pregnancy). By whose influence? What makes this cell adopt the forms it does if not the intelligent principle, acting through DNA and exercising the knowledge acquired through millions of years of development? Each particle, each portion of spiritual energy is individualised and follows its

own path, determined by free-will: the amœba reacts towards light, the fish decides to try and move on land and becomes the reptile, the amphibian takes to the air, the ape decides to build itself a shelter against the cold . . . and so on until evolution produces an Einstein or a Beethoven. And the more intelligence is developed, the more choice the free-will can exercise. Consideration of the billions of galaxies will show the limitless possibilities of evolvement their opportunities offer.

In modern man, the soul could be termed a closed-circuit of electro-magnetic energy, generated by what we call the mind. At first a particle charged with infinite energy, the mind must develop through evolvement. And for this it also has to develop free-will. Like a modern computer, the power station we call the mind learns, in the course of evolution, to accumulate data, and this accounts for the kind of process I have outlined above. But once the physiological evolvement of a species is complete, the computer has the data registered and repeats it mechanically at each new birth. From then on, the intelligence itself can be developed.

This is where consciousness begins. And at each new experience the computer registers more data and the opportunity to exercise free-will becomes proportionately greater. Each mind, each " power station " emits its own energy with its own wavelength. It is as though each of us were a private and separate radio station capable either of transmitting or receiving. How does this operate?

We know that the body acts according to " orders " telegraphed by the brain in the form of electrical impulses passing through the nervous system. What happens with thoughts and feelings is analogous. Each produces an impulse which in turn produces a wave of a certain type and length —thus the feeling of love produces the highest type of energy, with the fastest and subtlest wavelength, leaning towards the ultra-violet. Hatred, on the contrary produces a lower type of wavelength, tending towards the red end of the spectrum.

Since every feeling, thought and emotion thus has its physical expression in the kind of wave it emits, we dare to

affirm here that, apart from God, the intelligent principle itself, there is nothing that does not come under the heading of *physical* phenomena, nothing which has to be left in the realm only of philosophy, nothing which will not obey specific physical laws, not all of which have been discovered yet, of course. For I must emphasise again, the difference between what we call spiritual energy and material energy is nothing more than one of degrees in condensation.

Wladimir Leonidovitch Durov detected thought waves of the length of 1·8 millimetres during telepathic experiments in 1923. Parapsychologists are treading the same path today. And if in fact each thought and action (which is only the evolution of a thought, after all) produces its own electric wave with a wavelength and colour according to the kind of energy emitted by the original impulse of free-will creating it, then the traditional esoteric notion of the aura, whose colours vary according to its owner's personality, does not seem so far-fetched as once it did. " Life is an electrical phenomenon mediated by an infinite variety of chemical permutations," Dr. E. E. Suckling, Associate Professor of Medical Physics at the Downtown State Medical Centre, State University of New York, has written. I do not dispute it, but the definition can now be expanded into the " spiritual " sphere.

5. *Man's evolution is processed through constant incarnations which are but condensations and discondensations of his original energetic nature.*

The concept of reincarnation has always caused a certain repugnance to the Western mind, though over one billion people in the Orient have accepted it as a natural law for centuries. Partly, the reason lies in the possibility of " social degradation " in one incarnation as a sort of " punishment " for misdemeanours in another; partly it is the idea that a person now of a high status may not always have been so, both of them conceptions inimical to the highly developed Western ego! But the main stumbling block has always been the lack of remembrance of any past existence.

I unhesitatingly postulate that the *possibility* of reincarnation is verifiable through scientific method and therefore include it in our "working hypothesis", where it is vulnerable and welcome to observational attack. It is my conviction that the concept would manage to survive true scientific probing.

The main argument in favour is based not so much on proof as on logic and reason, much as the scientists affirm the supposition that intelligent life as we know it is not confined to this one planet.

I believe that, as DNA and the genes have "registered" in them all the process of evolution, so the intelligent and spiritual evolvement of the individual is imprinted in his "spiritual memory" The only difference between us here and "them up there" lies in the degree of condensation. If this is so, then why do we not remember our former incarnations?

Compared with the 50,000 years of our existence, our intellectual development is recent. The discovery of atomic energy is only about 30 years old; the formula that made it possible was first expressed by Einstein 60 years ago. And what is 60 years, what are 50,000 compared with the billions of light years that separate us from the quasars? But, during the tiny period of time in which our intelligence has begun to advance at last, our ethical and moral standards have already been left behind. Our capacity for producing and arranging thoughts may have improved; our capacity for love has not. All religions have failed, all social institutions and political structures have failed; we fought each other in the caves—and we are still fighting. . . . And this "backlog" of progress in love has inhibited the blossoming of higher sensitivity in the area of our cerebral cortex where all past experience, and thus all past incarnations, are registered. We have not, in short, yet evolved to the stage where our brain can "remember" all these past experiences, these former incarnations.

It is perhaps worth dwelling for a moment, though, on a discovery of Dr. Wilder Penfield of the Montreal Neuro-

logical Institute, reported in William L. Laurence's *New Frontiers of Science*. By stimulating the brains of human patients, Penfield, using tiny electrical currents, discovered "a new area of the cerebral cortex to which until now (1957) no function had been assigned". Patients " suddenly re-lived, as though it was actually happening again, long forgotten episodes of their childhood. Many patients stated that the experience brought back by the electrode was far more ' real ' than remembering, yet they were completely conscious of the present. There was a ' doubling ' of consciousness and yet the subject was aware of which was the here and now.

" How is this record of the past stored in the brain?" Dr. Penfield asked. " One may assume that at the time of the original experience, electrical potentials passed through the nerve cells and nerve connections of a recording mechanism in a specific, patterned sequence, and that some form of permanent facilitation preserves that sequence so that the ' record ' can be played at a later time, in a manner analogous to the replaying of a wire or tape recorder. But this remains a supposition."

It seems a reasonable supposition that this discovery may well be the key to the secret of reincarnation. Any day now, a scientist might, even as it were by accident, activate through an electrode an area of the brain, perhaps adjacent to Penfield's, which could recall past incarnations.

6. *Each action or thought expresses itself through electrical waves produced by man's energetical potential. Moral law has its physical expression in the conception that for every action there is a reaction. Man receives himself the result of the waves he emits. The law of reincarnation can thus be expressed : We are today the result of yesterday; tomorrow we shall be the result of today.*

7. *Each man is fully responsible for his actions. His progress through reincarnations will be faster or slower according to his own choice.*

8. *There is no race, no religion, no people in any sense
" chosen ". Each of us originates from the same source—
supreme energy—and is endowed with the same basic
potentials. Creation being continual, there are older and
younger spirits. This is one of the reasons for the different
stages of spiritual evolution we constantly witness on
Earth.*

9. *Miracles do not exist. Everything works according to laws
which are perfect. It is up to us, through evolution, to
discover them.*

10. *Jesus is the oldest and most evolved spirit that has ever
incarnated upon Earth. He was born, and died, the same
way as everybody else. His spiritual nature, or his dis-
condensed body, continues to live, as is the case with any
of us. The difference is in degree of evolvement. Universal
Religion says to all men : Each one of you will become a
Jesus one day, each one of you will be the carrier of a
torch to light a lower sphere, a planet whose stage of
evolvement will be similar to ours when Jesus came.
Jesus himself happens to be millions of years ahead of
us. The dynamics of the universe have it that those with
more light guide those with less, so Jesus is truly our
Lord, our Sun of love and wisdom. He reached this stage
by evolution; and one day we shall reach it too.*

Where, a lot of people ask, do all the apparitions of Jesus
come in? Evolvement is made possible through condensation
and discondensation, also called reincarnation, because when
the individualised personality in this spiritual, less condensed
state condenses itself, it takes on flesh, incarnates. What Jesus
did under special conditions was to condense his body to the
point of being the same as ours, but only on special occasions
and for a limited amount of time. Modern experiences of
materialisation rest on the same principle. For even " the
spirits " are material—though less condensed than we are.

ABOVE, LEFT: A child is baptized according to one of the many Umbanda rituals. ABOVE, RIGHT: There are those who combine sensationalism with primitive forces, such as this 'horse' of an Indian spiritual entity who brought this python onto the beach of the prosperous district of Leblon on Yemanjá night. BELOW: Black and white children, side by side, intone Umbanda chants at the 'Tenda Caboclo Mirim.'

ABOVE, LEFT: A worshipper, a young girl, is lifted from the sand by an 'Indian guide' after falling into trance. ABOVE, RIGHT: Dorval Ketzer, the son of German Catholic immigrants, is the 'Spiritual Director' of an Umbanda Association, and is one of the more cultured and responsible leaders of Umbanda in Brazil. BELOW, LEFT: The Temple of Universal Religion, the centre of charity as well as spiritual activity. BELOW, RIGHT: The Founder of the Temple of Universal Religion and the author of this book is seen here at the door of the Temple at one of the annual Christmas distributions.

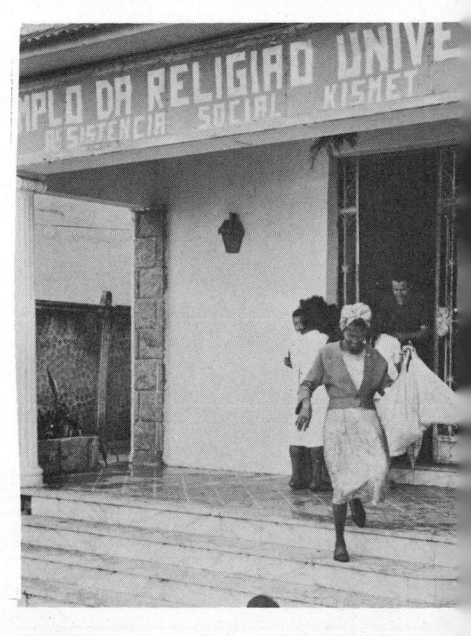

11. *Intelligence or intelligent life flourishes in as many billion galaxies as our imagination or science is able to detect. And many more. This planet is from one of the more inferior ones.*

12. *So-called spirit communications are nothing but the transmission of thought waves from the less condensed to the more condensed, through the perception of our nervous cells. Mediums have more sensitive nervous systems, capable of receiving and perceiving the faster wavelengths of the thoughts emitted by the spiritual entities. Just as, through evolvement, a previously "dead" area of the brain can now be stimulated to recall past material experience, and will one day no doubt be stimulated to recall past incarnations, so one day another area will be completely alive and sensitive to the presence and "speech" of spiritual entities. On that day, the question, Are you a medium? will become meaningless. Everybody will have the same powers as those we term mediums today, and the name will simply disappear. To ask the question would be like asking today: Are you a human being?*

Where does prayer fit into the picture formed by these twelve precepts? Prayer is the greatest, most effective catalyst of higher spiritual energy that we know. If it really " comes from the heart ", it concentrates unbelievable amounts of energy, which can be projected to a certain objective by higher spiritual entities, provided always that the motive is according to universal laws and stems basically from love.

To return to the subject of spirit communication, one of the main reasons why attempts to analyse this from a scientific viewpoint have failed lies in the fact that no two mediums are the same and thus no phenomenon ever exactly repeats itself. Observations with only one medium have been successfully attempted by several scientists during the past century, but they are vulnerable to the accusation of fraud. Yet if science were to apply its enormous knowledge of electronics, biochemistry and nuclear physics systematically to the discovery of the spiritual nature of man, accepting as a working

hypothesis the tenets of Universal Religion, it could well make a breakthrough in the understanding of our nature and our predicament equal in impact to the discovery of how to split the atom.

On the Brazilian scene Universal Religion represents the first real effort of unification of the Spiritist movement, not through any kind of " Pope " or any imposed structure, but simply by harmonising the various currents of thought and of spiritual principle in conformity with the laws of nature, and not with preconceived ideas or ancient religious traditions, however valuable.

On the broader, world scene, Universal Religion presents a unified field theory capable of harmonising religion and science by giving them both a common ground and purpose. Dogmas and miracles are "out" and man emerges free to conquer the Universe through love and wisdom, not through missiles or bombs.

Religion, to have any meaning today, must take into consideration such diversities as the energy of the quasars, the millions of billions of possible worlds in the Universe, and the whole complex range of scientific knowledge here on Earth, as well as the moral and spiritual values by which the Intelligent Principle works. On a future world inhabited by a super-civilisation, religion will have an expression and a form beyond our present understanding. Yet the basic principles of Universal Religion will still apply, much as basic arithmetic still holds good despite the existence of computers. . . .

Let us end this study with a sentence of one of the most brilliant men of the century, Fred Hoyle:

" It is true that we must not accept a theory on the basis of an emotional preference. But it is not an emotional preference to attempt to establish a theory that would place us in a position to obtain complete understanding of the Universe. The stakes are high and, win or lose, are worth playing for."